The Makings of a Poet

The Makings of a Poet

VANESSA IVEY

THE MAKINGS OF A POET

iUniverse books may be ordered through booksellers or by contacting:

iUniverse
1663 Liberty Drive
Bloomington, IN 47403
www.iuniverse.com
844-349-9409

ISBN: 978-1-6632-2108-7 (sc)
ISBN: 978-1-6632-2107-0 (e)

Print information available on the last page.

iUniverse rev. date: 04/20/2021

"Going in Circles"

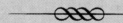

Crowd Full of Mothers

Empty manifestations and prophecies My prayers go unanswered once again I've waited so many years…

To hear the words, 'Your wait has come to an end. Here is your child. Your womb has been healed within'

But no…I hear nothing

Nothing but sentiments and proverbs

To puff up my hope

Then reality emerges

And a little more than before, my soul dies

Every moment that my womb remains closed feels like a peruse through hell

I've heard and believed so many magnificent and beautiful things about you

And I even tried to alter my life's view to be congruent with the empty headed masses

Yes, I do have so many blessings

And my gratitude may be eclipsed, but it's not missing

But the one thing I desire to death

Is withheld by life, maybe even attested Disgrace humbles me in a crowd full of mothers Haven't I been washed? Haven't I been made clean?

Hasn't every evil thing been burned or beaten out of me? What remains is the dull ache of pain

Unmade memories of swollen feet, a rounding belly and watching my family grow from two to three

I presume I'm babbling again

Vanessa Ivey

Trying to vent some abstract emotional truth

I feel anger swelling up inside me

I was born a slave

Created only to find an idea of God and bring it praise Dedicated by my family at such an early age Appointed before I could choose my own way

Cursed with the insatiable passion to bear and birth a child

Before I submit to the grave

A very great and precious promise remains in my heart

But my heart is on my sleeve

And I've had to pick up the broken pieces of life in the dark

I have experienced Your love so clearly

But now I've lived and I understand To know You is to know pain Whether an ideal or a reality

You cause the eyes to cry seven seas

The universe loves a stubborn heart and

I will not surrender my dream

War Crimes

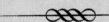

I was born in the deep end

*Icy cold waters you could not breathe in Only choices were to
     rise or to sink in Blackness all around*

Couldn't tell up from down

Sad voices wanting me to drown

I made it out alive

*Don't know how to be happy Only know how to survive When
     there is no war*

A soldier just lies...pretending to be

Lies...waiting to be Happiness is not attained It is realized

Survival is not a skill

It's a sentence for someone else's crimes

The Throne

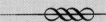

There was no preview to loving you

No map, no counselor, no teacher

To show me what to do

Concrete walls, deep oceans and dry deserts

I fought my way through

All with the intention to somehow siphon love from you

I have an inverse relationship between my insecurities and my pride

For in order for one to live, the other must die

The former forces me to covet love

And insecurities don't care if I beg for, borrow or steal love

The latter is fulfilled only by your adoration and unprovoked love

Received as a tribute to my power - but hidden from the public, really my lack thereof

Each day is a day of Russian roulette

But in this game of thrones disappointment is always the winning bet

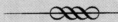

Spoken by a Survivor

God made her and you raped her

Stripped her of all her hopes and dreams and left her with illusions of forever

Now her heart is severed

Bleeding out in the sheets

The same sheets you left her alone in, day after day, week after week

She's asking herself, 'How did I become so weak?'

Even though her heart needed saving, her love for you wouldn't let her speak

She gave you her soul...and because of your childhood complexities,

like never seeing your father love your mother, it lead to grown man insecurities

But her soul...

Instead of reciprocating love

You just demanded more control

You pushed her away

But even in her loneliness and doubt she stayed

Even after all the videos, all the messages of you being disloyal, that she played I was there when she told you 'please don't make my love for you turn to hate' You gave her a kiss and said 'ok'

Then proceeded to steal every piece of dignity she had left to take

Oh, but life never forgets

And you can't out live fate

You will see her pain again, somehow, someway

And life will make you remember her face

I used to be her

I'm the her after you

Like a city leveled by a hurricane When the Red Cross comes through I learned so much from you

Truth be told...I'll always...love you

But what you need to do is rarely what you want to do

Sometimes it feels impossible to do

But when I am weak

I become strong

I am the one that helps me through

I wish you love and happiness

I still cry sometimes because I could never forget

I just accepted the fact that in life

I'm going east

And you know...some people go west

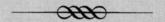

The Beginnings of a Lie

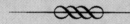

I know it's time

But I'm having second thoughts

You've already been so patient and I hate to keep you waiting in the dark

I'm crying in my mind

But a smile is all you see

As you kiss and touch my body thinking you're arousing me

All I can think about is my childhood villain and what he stole from me

Sitting in that black room wishing I could disappear

He kept touching and touching

I know he felt my tears Okay back to reality Fifteen years later

I'm not a child anymore and my nightmares should have faded

But they haven't

And all the love that you've given me hasn't even made a dent

Into the pain of that secret I've tried to relent Shame, guilt and confusion cloud my mind But I fear if I don't oblige you

You'll think loving me was a waste of time

So I take off my clothes and climb on top of you

Trying my hardest not to remember what he used to do I hear you moaning in bliss while it feels as if I'm dying But it's too late to retreat now

So I just remain silently crying

I whisper 'stop' under my breath

Deliberately keeping it from reaching your ears

It's not your fault that I've kept that part of me a secret for all these years

Why can't you tell that something is wrong

You say that you love me

Can't you sense when you're hurting me accidentally or purposely

You don't have a clue

I am a good pretender

But I thought I'd finally found someone to whom the real me

I could totally surrender

Please, please stop is what my heart is saying But my mind says joy comes at the price of pain I don't want to lose you

So I'll do what it takes

Even if I have to relive the tragedies of yesterday

Suddenly my hold on reality is leaving And I revisit myself at six years old Afraid and wondering why I was bleeding

He said, "all girls bleed, it's the natural cycle of life"

But now I know why he only played that game at night

I was yanked back into reality when I noticed the light had been turned on

Then I heard you gently whisper to me "what's wrong" Quickly believing I could never share this pain with you My mind raced for a believable lie

Something to make sense

Some reason why

Then I just said it…

"I'm so happy right now that I started to cry".

Lust in Love

Lust says right now, love says I'll wait Lust says you're mine, love says in time Love is patient, love is kind

Lust has no control of time

It needs you now, there is no later

Love moves slow because its weight is greater

They both would look the same in the dark

And they both have torn great kingdoms apart The sun and the moon both depart their light Radiant and brilliant, but each of a different type Alluring, tempting, deceiving I'll say

Moonlight dancing in the shadows that come after the day

Protection, truth and forgiveness stand long during the day when the sun is strong

But desire, passion and emotion emerge when the moon becomes

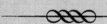

My Great Escape

Every time I see you

You give me life

You have a peep hole to my soul

They couldn't separate us with the sharpest knife

I promise to never feed you a lie

I promise to only reflect to you light

Of your loyalty and love I will never take advantage Our passion is something I'll never take for granted As the moonlight hugs the curves of the ocean

I feel your gaze holding me, intoxicating me in slow motion

I'm drunk off our love

And I'm high off our life

Ever since that cold day in November

I haven't thought twice

About greeting eternity with you by my side

I crown you king and as your queen

I want to be your joy and pride

My commitment to you flows deeper than the Nile

If I thought I could still walk away unscathed

I would be in denial

I jumped all in for you

But you didn't let me stay there alone

You plunged in too

I carefully broke my ravished heart into two

And surrendered a bleeding half to you

Can you mend a heart you didn't break, I ask

And can you replace the trust that you didn't take

I vow to heal you, help in your transformation and reveal you

You whispered as you softly kissed my face

"Your love can never be replaced'

All the tears that stained my face

You have erased and by bringing me joy, you helped me make my great escape

From the prison of the mind

The bars grew impenetrable over time

But you held the key to release me

And now I dance in celebration over what's mine

Peace, freedom and the rest of our time

Together, I'm betting on forever

Your eyes asked me will I ever leave

I laid on your chest and whispered to your heart 'never'

Now you share in the thoughts that pulsate through my mind

Just know that I cherish you

Soul, body and mind

Finally Ready

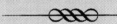

One day I realized that everything I thought I knew

I never really knew at all

I thought I was mature

But I was just learning to crawl

Really just beginning to fall

I was caught up in a game that only I was playing

To make it worse

I thought I was winning

How lonely my life must have been

But I never knew

I feel it now...stalking me

As soon as the forgiving noise of company is over

Then comes the cruelty of my silence The noisy combustion of my thoughts Humility mixed with defiance Trapped...lost... wounded is what I am I bandaged up my own heart

But I have been bleeding from within

The world can no longer see it

But I am not blind to my own pain

I desperately tried to have faith

I shared my delusions with others so boldly

But I walked into an ambush

And what hurts the most

Is that I walked in solely

It would have made no difference if we were together

Hand in hand I would have stayed devoted to you

No matter the weather

But you left me

You left me in the storm

You took my love and deserted me

When I needed your arms

Or maybe...probably...you were never there

I made my hopes into you

And I sent myself all of those prayers

I hear whispers that against your love any comparison pales

I think that I am just afraid to let you fail

Secret humiliations can heal in silence

But many opinions compound public heartbreak Now those that don't know me judge me for trying Trying to heal, trying to breathe, just simply trying to be

Where are you now, God, and will you ever answer any of my whys? I marvel at the capacity of the human mind to lie

To itself and to the lost child behind someone else's eyes

Vanessa Ivey

Only Pieces

I can never dry my eyes behind you

Your smile hid so many lies

Still I lived and breathed for you

Now I grieve and bleed because of you

You promised me the world

To make my friends jealous of my big beautiful smile All you've done is fail me and bring me trial after trial Yet in all this tragedy my heart still cleaves to you

I lie awake feeling as if every breath is for you

I watched as all the love letters stopped The texts became shorter and shorter The kisses came fewer and fewer

The biggest mistake was making love with you

Did you turn into a liar

Or were you always impersonating the truth

I wanted to have a child with you

Now I barely want to share a picture with you

My souls still craves you

But all trust is gone

So is my beautiful future

Now I just move along waiting for the future

You turned me into a woman I never wanted to be again

Isolated, obsessed, jealous and bent on revenge

I begged for loyalty and honesty

All I got was lie after secret after secret after lie

When I tried to walk away

You'd just lie again to make me stay

I'm trapped in your illusion

But you, yourself, I cannot trace

Who will deliver me from this wretched life

All of our laughter decayed into strife

To a figment of my imagination I swore my life! Now all I'm left with is pieces…

Pieces that when put together only build a lie

I would have rathered died than to face this truth alone

But death wasn't meant to be

I was forced to empty this cup of our hopeless dreams

What a bitter concoction Our love potion was toxic Even now, I love you still Because a rose is still a rose

Even after the last petal is peeled

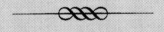

More Than Love

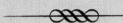

A real man knows how to hold a woman

How to reassure her of things that she already knows

He knows how to cultivate her garden

And never let weeds of distrust grow

He speaks to her in the language of a king Sealing their union with more than a ring Despite his imperfections his royalty shines He is lord over many men

But to her he gives and takes his time

Life has broadened his intellect And his intelligence is of no match Though he is dumbfounded by her beauty He allows her soul to roam his mind

As he falls into her arms to relax

He admires her body for much more than sex

A real woman does more than stand beside her man

She positions herself to support his weaknesses

Gently reminding him that he can When the world is on his shoulders She knows how to free his mind And lift every boulder

When she slips on her gown

She zips up her vest

The world is a war zone

For the black man at best

She would never leave his side

His strength is her pride

Only she sees what's deepest inside

She's embraced the failure of her man

And therefore has enabled him to win

She kisses him straight through to the inside

As she whispers that everything will be alright

It reaches the little boy that every man has locked away inside

She sees him...in him and nourishes him

Like a mother does a child

His hands are her home

And in her eyes is the reflection of his soul

There is no sacrifice too great

There is no leap that both of them would not make She is the thread that holds together all of his dreams He is the script to every one of her scenes

Love is not a big enough word to hold all that they feel

But it's the only word that makes any of this real

Her last words will be, 'my love don't let go of peace and happiness'

He'll reply, 'how could I have been so blessed to find a woman that loved me up until her last breath. Now my love you go on to rest. Happiness will come and go, but peace I will not find again until my death'

And so was the parting of the sky from the sea

The bird from its wings and today

You from me

The Little Blue Box

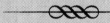

Oh, how I wanted that little blue box

How my heart ached for it so

Ever since I can remember, I dreamed I'd show

Some others had one or two

Maybe even four or more

The boxes looked so pretty nestled in the arms of the people

As they came and as they would go

Some carried them carefully as they should

Others dragged them along wishing they could

Be like me...empty handed with not one box to show

*It seemed I was all alone in the world Everywhere I looked I
could see the blue boxes Displayed like gold*

I cried out, 'Dear father, where is my box of gold?'

*That little blue box means more to me than anything else I
know*

Why have you forgotten me, why have you pained my heart so?

*I feel so ashamed that I have no little blue box, no box of gold
to show*

If my tears would turn into boxes

A mountain of treasure I would hold

As I walked empty handed down the path of life

I fell in love with someone who had two blue boxes

One on each side

How I envied those blue boxes

I so desperately wanted one of my own

To think back on it now, it was a long time before my father picked up the phone

There were a lot of questions that had built up over time But the only one I could muster was the original one Father, where is my blue box, didn't you get me one?

His answer changed my life, although it took quite a while

He said, 'no, I never designed a blue box for you my special, special child'

As my heart began to sink even deeper into my chest

He said, 'for you dear child, I did my very best'

I chuckled in my disbelief, though I could hardly stay afloat in my present grief

'You see when it came to you, no ordinary blue box would do. I designed a diamond chest with rubies that show through. The wait, my dear, has been for you.

It outweighed your strength and it's heaviness would have been too much for you. I have given you my treasure for the whole world to see how

I love you and what you mean to me.

But until you can carry it, it must remain safe with me.

Remember, it doesn't have to be in your arms to be a part of your destiny.'

In gratitude mixed with heartache and perseverance mixed with broken pride

I continued on my journey knowing that someday I would smile as I held my child

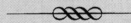

Naked and Saved

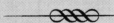

Naked…

Naked is what I've been for you

My undressed soul has brought down what used to be aloof

I've mirrored more than my reflection to you

My highly guarded matrix, my fortress has been yours to peruse

I had the power to remain unseen and misunderstood

But under the spotlight of your analyzation, with no certainties, I stood

Wanting to be received

But not pushing my way

Suffering to be loved and taken off of display

But the longer I stayed exposed the brighter I shone

Until my light overpowered your light

And I was the brightest in the room

Self-realization is the greatest illumination

My soul shone brilliantly

As time walked on, it no longer mattered what you could see

My soul uncovered my eyes For the first time in my life I could see

The way I looked in the light was so beautiful to me

I stepped off of the stage and into the world

Hoping that by looking at me

In themselves others could believe

Somehow I realized that this was a precious version of me

And that something so valuable would inevitably attract thieves
Then for a moment I turned back and thought of you
I wondered...were you able to see? Then I knew it didn't matter
I had finally lost you and found me

Vanessa Ivey

Printed in the United States
by Baker & Taylor Publisher Services